INSIDE THE NFL

PHILADELPHIA EAGLES

BY ROBERT COOPER

abdobooks.com

Published by Abdo Publishing, a division of ABDO, PO Box 398166, Minneapolis, Minnesota 55439.

Printed in the United States of America, North Mankato, Minnesota
022019
092019

THIS BOOK CONTAINS RECYCLED MATERIALS

Cover: Ron Jenkins/AP Images
Interior Photos: Peter Read Miller/AP Images, 5; Bruce Kluckhorn/AP Images, 7; Jeff Roberson/AP Images, 9; Perry Knotts/AP Images, 10; AP Images, 13; NFL Photos/AP Images, 17, 19, 29, 43; Al Messerschmidt/AP Images, 21; G. Paul Burnett/AP Images, 23; Bettmann/Getty Images, 25; Amy Sancetta/AP Images, 27; David Stluka/AP Images, 31; Mark Lennihan/AP Images, 32; Evan Vucci/AP Images, 35; Brian Garfinkel/AP Images, 39; Ryan Kang/AP Images, 41

Editor: Patrick Donnelly
Series Designer: Craig Hinton

Library of Congress Control Number: 2018965949

Publisher's Cataloging-in-Publication Data

Names: Cooper, Robert, author.
Title: Philadelphia Eagles / by Robert Cooper
Description: Minneapolis, Minnesota: Abdo Publishing, 2020 | Series: Inside the NFL | Includes online resources and index.
Identifiers: ISBN 9781532118616 (lib. bdg.) | ISBN 9781532172793 (ebook) | ISBN 9781644941140 (pbk.)
Subjects: LCSH: Philadelphia Eagles (Football team)--Juvenile literature. | National Football League--Juvenile literature. | Football teams--Juvenile literature. | American football--Juvenile literature.
Classification: DDC 796.33264--dc23

TABLE OF CONTENTS

CHAPTER 1

CHAMPIONS AT LAST

The Philadelphia Eagles had their hands full heading into Super Bowl LII in 2018. The New England Patriots entered the game as the defending Super Bowl champions. Behind head coach Bill Belichick and quarterback Tom Brady, they had won five Super Bowls. Only the Pittsburgh Steelers had won more in their history.

The Eagles did not have the same pedigree. This was only their third Super Bowl, and their first since losing to New England in 2005. Philadelphia also didn't have much experience at the quarterback position. The Eagles' starting quarterback, Carson Wentz, suffered a season-ending knee injury in December. That meant backup Nick Foles had to take over. So far, Foles had survived as the Eagles held on

Quarterback Nick Foles came up big for the Eagles under the bright lights of the Super Bowl.

EAGLES

NICK FOLES

Nick Foles took over for injured Philadelphia quarterback Carson Wentz late in the 2018 regular season. Though he was the Eagles' backup quarterback, fans in Philadelphia were familiar with Foles. He had been drafted by Philadelphia in 2012 and led the team to the playoffs in 2013 as the starting quarterback. But after struggling in 2014, he was traded to the St. Louis Rams. He spent one season in St. Louis and then another with the Kansas City Chiefs before he returned to back up Wentz in Philadelphia in 2017.

to beat the Atlanta Falcons and Minnesota Vikings in the playoffs. But the Patriots would be Foles's toughest challenge yet.

The game started well for Philadelphia. Foles completed passes to many different receivers. The score was tied 3–3 when Foles hit wide receiver Alshon Jeffery for the game's first touchdown.

Late in the second quarter, the Eagles led 15–12. At the two-minute warning, the Eagles took over at their own 30-yard line with one more chance to get on the scoreboard before halftime. On their third play, Foles hit running back Corey Clement with a short pass. Clement broke free and took the ball all the way to the New England 8-yard line before he was brought down.

Three plays later, the Eagles had the ball on the Patriots 1-yard line. It was fourth down. Philadelphia was having

Eagles wide receiver Alshon Jeffery (17) hauls in a touchdown pass from Foles in the first quarter of the Super Bowl.

trouble getting past the Patriots defense and into the end zone. But head coach Doug Pederson didn't want to settle for a field goal. He knew that every point would count against a high-scoring team such as the Patriots. And he knew just the play to call.

Philadelphia lined up in its regular formation. Then Foles moved over to the right side of the offensive line. The snap went directly to Clement. He ran left, then flipped the ball to tight end Trey Burton coming back the other way. Foles, meanwhile, had zipped out of the backfield and was open near the goal line. Burton threw a perfect pass and Foles reeled it in for a touchdown. The play they called the "Philly Special" gave the Eagles a 22–12 halftime lead.

"I trust my players, I trust my coaches, and I trust my instincts," Pederson said.

In the second half, each team's offense came out on fire. The Patriots took the kickoff and marched down the field. Brady hit tight end Rob Gronkowski in the end zone to make it 22–19. But the Eagles drove right back down the field. Foles and Clement connected again on third down, this time for a 22-yard touchdown to restore Philadelphia's 10-point lead.

Brady threw another touchdown pass. The Eagles came back with a Jake Elliott field goal to give them a 32–26 lead. But that didn't last long. Brady hooked up with Gronkowski again for a touchdown. The extra point gave New England its first lead of the game, 33–32.

Foles responded with the drive of a lifetime. Taking over at their own 25 with just under 10 minutes to play, the Eagles soon faced third down with six yards to go for a first down. Foles calmly hit tight end Zach Ertz for seven yards. On their next series of downs, the Eagles found themselves staring at another 4th-and-1 decision, this time at their own 45.

Foles catches a touchdown pass from tight end Trey Burton on the "Philly Special" trick play late in the first half.

Ever the gambler, Pederson opted to go for it again. Foles rewarded his coach's faith by converting on another short pass to Ertz, and the drive continued. Then, on 3rd-and-7 at the New England 11, Foles went with the hot hand and found Ertz, who made the catch on the run. Ertz was tripped up but still managed to reach the ball across the goal line to give Philadelphia a 38–33 lead.

Philadelphia head coach Doug Pederson holds the Lombardi Trophy after the Eagles won their first Super Bowl title.

The Eagles couldn't celebrate quite yet, though. A little more than two minutes remained on the clock, plenty of time for Brady to orchestrate one more long drive. On second down, Eagles defensive end Brandon Graham broke through the line and sacked Brady, who fumbled. Eagles teammate Derek Barnett recovered, but the game still wasn't over. New England's defense held the Eagles to a field goal, giving Philadelphia a 41–33 lead with 1:05 to play. Once again, Brady would have the opportunity to play hero.

AN OFFENSIVE OUTBURST

Super Bowl LII was a thrilling game that came down to the wire. It will long be remembered for its historic offensive numbers. The Eagles and Patriots combined for a record 1,151 offensive yards. Tom Brady set the record for most passing yards in a postseason game with 505. That was key to New England scoring 33 points, which was the most ever scored by a losing team in a Super Bowl. Foles threw for 373 yards and three touchdowns while catching another scoring pass to win the game's Most Valuable Player (MVP) Award.

With nine seconds left, the Patriots reached midfield. Now they had time for one last play: a Hail Mary pass. Brady took the snap and launched a high pass toward the end zone. The ball fell to the turf, and the Eagles were Super Bowl champions for the first time ever. It was a reward for the team and fans who had been disappointed so many times. This was their time to celebrate.

CHAPTER 2

THE EARLY YEARS

The Frankford Yellow Jackets were a National Football League (NFL) team located in the suburbs of Philadelphia that folded in 1931. Businessmen Bert Bell and Lud Wray wanted to fill the void left by their departure. They led an investment group that purchased the rights to an NFL franchise in the Philadelphia market for $2,500. The Philadelphia Eagles began play in 1933.

Pro football in Pennsylvania underwent more changes in 1940. Pittsburgh Steelers owner Art Rooney sold his stake in the team to Alexis Thompson. Rooney then bought half interest in the Eagles. But one year later, Rooney returned to Pittsburgh. Rooney took Bell with him and swapped franchises with Thompson.

Bert Bell, coach and owner of the Eagles, talks to his squad on July 26, 1939.

The two teams would soon work together in a different way. During World War II (1939–1945), fewer men were available to play football because they had enlisted in the armed forces. So for the 1943 season, the two Pennsylvania teams merged and played under the name "Phil-Pitt Steagles."

The Phil-Pitt Steagles split up after the 1943 season. Earle "Greasy" Neale returned to his role as head coach of the Philadelphia Eagles. Under Neale's leadership, the Eagles became a winning team for the first time on their own.

First-round draft pick Steve Van Buren took over at halfback in 1944. The Eagles went 7–1–2 to finish in second place in the NFL's Eastern Conference behind the New York Giants.

Philadelphia contended for the title in the years ahead. Future Hall of Famers Van Buren, end Pete Pihos, and center/linebacker

SHARING RESOURCES

The Philadelphia Eagles and Pittsburgh Steelers shared everything in the 1943 season playing as the Phil-Pitt Steagles. Earle "Greasy" Neale of the Eagles and Walt Kiesling of the Steelers served as co-coaches. The roster was split among available players from the two teams. The combined team produced a 5–4–1 record. The winning record was something the Eagles had not accomplished in their first 10 years on their own.

Alex Wojciechowicz led the way. The Eagles held second place for three straight seasons. However, without playoffs, only the division winners moved on to the NFL Championship Game.

Van Buren led the NFL in rushing yards and touchdowns four times in five years, beginning with his second season in 1945. He helped make Philadelphia the highest-scoring team in the NFL that season. However, it was the tough Eagles defense that eventually put the team on top.

The Eagles and Steelers were connected again in 1947. The two Pennsylvania teams tied for first place in the Eastern Conference at 8–4. This set up a playoff to determine who would face the Chicago Cardinals in the NFL Championship Game. The Eagles allowed the Steelers only seven first downs, while Philadelphia quarterback Tommy Thompson threw two touchdown passes in a 21–0 shutout victory.

The Cardinals spoiled the Eagles' first championship game appearance. Playing at home in Comiskey Park, the Cardinals led by two touchdowns three times. Each time Philadelphia came back to get within seven points. The Eagles, however, were never able to erase the deficit and lost 28–21.

The next year the Eagles shut out four opponents on the way to a 9–2–1 record. That was good enough for another

STEVE VAN BUREN

Steve Van Buren was the leading offensive player on back-to-back Eagles championship teams in 1948 and 1949. He scored the winning touchdown in 1948.

Orphaned as a young boy in Honduras, he became one of the game's great underdog stories. Van Buren moved to New Orleans to live with his grandparents and was unable to make his high school football team as a 125-pound sophomore. In his senior year, Van Buren landed a scholarship to play football at Louisiana State University.

Van Buren played halfback but with the toughness of a fullback. The five-time NFL All-Pro led the league in rushing, scoring, and kick returning in 1945, his second season in Philadelphia. Van Buren played eight seasons in the NFL, all with the Eagles. He was enshrined in the Pro Football Hall of Fame in 1965.

berth in the NFL Championship Game. The game was a rematch with the Cardinals, but this time at Shibe Park in Philadelphia.

A heavy snowstorm pounded Philadelphia that day, making it nearly impossible to pass the ball. The teams combined to complete just five passes, while three other attempts were intercepted. Finally, in the fourth quarter, Van Buren plowed his way into the end zone from 5 yards out, and the Eagles earned their first NFL title with a 7–0 win.

The Eagles chose Chuck Bednarik with the first pick of the 1949 NFL Draft. Bednarik played linebacker and center at the

Eagles players shiver on the sideline during the snowy 1948 NFL title game victory over the Cardinals.

University of Pennsylvania. He joined an Eagles team that won its third straight NFL Eastern Conference title in 1949.

The 1949 team, arguably the greatest in Eagles history, went 11–1. The Eagles led the league in scoring with 364 points and gave up a league-low 134 points. They were especially dominant late in the season. The New York Giants failed to score a touchdown against the Eagles in two meetings to end the regular season. Then Philadelphia shut out the Los Angeles Rams 14–0 to claim their second straight NFL title. Van Buren ran for a team-playoff record 196 yards as the Eagles became the first team to win back-to-back NFL titles by shutout.

CHAPTER 3

UPS AND DOWNS

Chuck Bednarik had the reputation of being one of the toughest players in the NFL from the late 1940s to the early 1960s. He played a central role in the Eagles' 1960 NFL championship. The last of the league's full-time, two-way players, Bednarik was regarded as one of the league's best centers as well as an outstanding linebacker. He was on the field for 58 of the 60 minutes on December 26 when Philadelphia faced the Green Bay Packers in the NFL Championship Game.

The Eagles scored the only touchdown of the first three quarters when quarterback Norm Van Brocklin, the NFL's MVP that year, found Tommy McDonald with a 35-yard touchdown pass in the second quarter. Philadelphia led 10–6

Chuck Bednarik played center and linebacker for the Eagles in the 1950s and early 1960s.

60

entering the fourth quarter. That's when things picked up. Packers quarterback Bart Starr hit Max McGee with a 7-yard touchdown pass to put Green Bay in front 13–10. Philadelphia's Ted Dean returned the ensuing kickoff 58 yards, setting up his own 5-yard run for the go-ahead touchdown with 5:21 to play.

Trailing 17–13, Starr led the Packers down the field for one last shot. Nearing the Eagles' end zone, Green Bay running back Jim Taylor appeared to have an opening. Bednarik quickly closed it. He stopped Taylor at the 8-yard line and held him down a couple seconds longer to make sure the clock ran out before the Packers could run another play. For the first time in 11 years, the Eagles were NFL champions.

The Eagles went 10–4 the next year but finished in second place, missing the playoffs. It turned out to be the start of a 17-year postseason drought. The 1966 team went 9–5 for their only winning record in that stretch. The trouble started when the 1962 team was wiped out by a series of injuries and went 3–10–1. In just two years, the Eagles had dropped from league champions to last place in the division.

In the 1970s, the Eagles started adding the pieces that would allow the team to be successful again. Wide receiver Harold Carmichael, the team's all-time receiving leader, was

Dick Vermeil led the Eagles to four playoff appearances and a Super Bowl in his time as their coach, from 1976 to 1982.

drafted in 1971. All-Pro linebacker Bill Bergey came to the team in a trade with the Cincinnati Bengals in 1974. Dick Vermeil left the University of California, Los Angeles (UCLA) to become head coach of the Eagles in 1976. A trade with the Los Angeles Rams brought quarterback Ron Jaworski to Philadelphia in 1977. The playoff drought was about to end in spectacular fashion.

The Eagles were improving in 1978, Vermeil's third season as coach. The team had a 6–5 record when it went to the

Meadowlands to play the New York Giants on November 19. The Giants led 17–12 in the final minute. The Eagles were out of timeouts. All the Giants needed to do was have quarterback Joe Pisarcik take the snap and kneel to down the ball. Then the clock would run out.

The Giants took a different approach—and they paid the price. Pisarcik turned to hand off to fullback Larry Csonka. But as Pisarcik reached out, the ball hit Csonka's hip and bounced free. Pisarcik scrambled to retrieve the ball. It bounced again, this time into the hands of Eagles cornerback Herman Edwards.

Edwards took off on an improbable 26-yard fumble return for the game-winning touchdown with 20 seconds left. The play, which came to be known as

TIMELY HIT

Bill Bergey credited fellow Eagles linebacker Frank LeMaster with setting up "the Miracle at the Meadowlands." The fumble return in the final minute allowed Philadelphia to edge the New York Giants 19–17 in 1978 and sent the team on its way to a playoff berth.

In 2009 Bergey told Comcast Sports that LeMaster had fired through the line and hit Giants quarterback Joe Pisarcik as he took a knee on the previous play. The teams started fighting and had to be separated. On the next play, Pisarcik tried to hand off instead of kneeling again to end the game. When he did, Pisarcik and fullback Larry Csonka fumbled the exchange. This allowed Herman Edwards to come up with the ball and run it in for the winning touchdown.

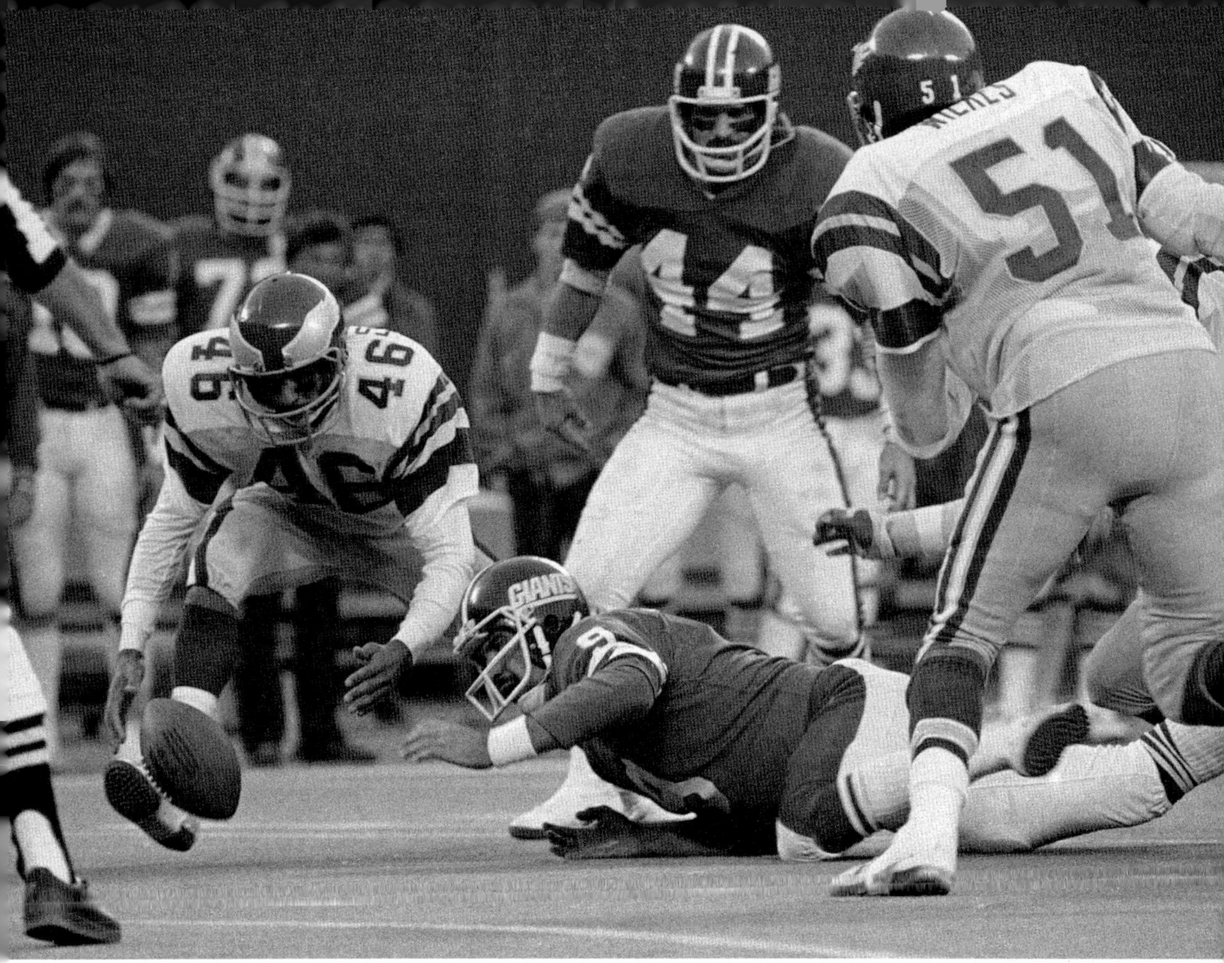

Eagles cornerback Herman Edwards (46) picks up a fumble by Giants quarterback Joe Pisarcik in the "Miracle at the Meadowlands" game in 1978.

"the Miracle at the Meadowlands," turned around the Eagles' fortunes. It meant the difference between an 8–8 finish and a 9–7 season. It was Philadelphia's first winning record in a dozen years and its first playoff appearance since 1960.

The 1978 season started a stretch of four straight in which the Eagles made the playoffs. The 1980 team was the most

ONE-TWO PUNCH

The Eagles' all-time leading receiver and second all-time leading rusher played together for seven seasons from 1977 to 1983. Harold Carmichael caught 589 passes for 8,978 yards with the Eagles from 1971 to 1983. Wilbert Montgomery rushed for 6,538 yards for Philadelphia from 1977 to 1984.

accomplished of those playoff squads. It set a club record with 12 wins. Then the Eagles defeated the East Division rival Dallas Cowboys 20–7 in the National Football Conference (NFC) Championship Game in Philadelphia.

The Eagles advanced to Super Bowl XV against the Oakland Raiders. But it wouldn't be a happy ending for Philadelphia. Jaworski threw three interceptions, while Oakland quarterback Jim Plunkett threw for three touchdowns in the game. The Raiders beat the Eagles 27–10.

Philadelphia began to struggle even before its run of playoff appearances ended. The Eagles started the 1981 season 6–0. But they lost six of their remaining 10 games before losing in the wild-card round of the playoffs. Vermeil resigned at the end of the 1982 season. His departure signaled that a new era of Eagles football was about to begin.

Running back Wilbert Montgomery was a key player on Philadelphia's 1980 NFC Championship team.

CHAPTER 4

ON THE DEFENSIVE

The Eagles teams of the late 1980s and mid-1990s were known for their tough defenses. That was not surprising since two of their head coaches during that time, Buddy Ryan and Ray Rhodes, were known as defensive innovators.

Ryan had been the defensive coordinator for the dominant 1985 Chicago Bears championship team. Upon taking over as Eagles coach the next year, he led the team to the playoffs in 1988, 1989, and 1990. Following four mediocre seasons under Rich Kotite, Rhodes took over in 1995. He had been the San Francisco 49ers' defensive coordinator. In his first season, he was named NFL Coach of the Year while leading the Eagles to the playoffs. The team repeated that effort in 1996.

The Eagles' Reggie White sacks Dolphins quarterback Dan Marino in 1987.

MARINO
13

THE FOG BOWL

A thick fog moved in off Lake Michigan after the start of the 1988 divisional playoff between the Bears and Eagles. This severely limited visibility during Chicago's 20–12 victory. In the press box, announcers could no longer accurately describe the action on the field because they could not see it. On the field, the players could not see much more than 10 or 15 yards away.

"When that fog rolled in, you might as well close your eyes and close up the shop," Philadelphia quarterback Randall Cunningham said 20 years later. "That was it. We could probably have had the whole team on field and people wouldn't have known. Maybe that's what we should have done." Once the fog had settled in, each team could manage to score only one field goal in the second half.

But for all their regular-season success, the Eagles won only a single playoff game under the two defensive gurus. After falling to the host Chicago Bears 20–12 in the divisional round in 1988, they lost wild-card games at home the next two years and Ryan was fired.

Things didn't improve much under Kotite. Early in the 1991 season, starting quarterback Randall Cunningham and his backup, Jim McMahon, were lost due to injuries. The Eagles needed five quarterbacks just to get through the first half of the season with a 3–5 record. But the defense produced another 10-win season. The Eagles led the NFL in sacks, takeaways, rushing yardage allowed, passing yardage allowed, and total defense. Three-fourths of Philadelphia's talented defensive line—tackle

Eagles coach Buddy Ryan walks on the sideline during Philadelphia's 20–12 "Fog Bowl" playoff loss at Chicago on December 31, 1988.

Jerome Brown and ends Reggie White and Clyde Simmons—played in the Pro Bowl.

The Eagles went 11–5 in 1992 and defeated the New Orleans Saints in the wild-card playoff round. The Eagles scored the game's final 29 points, 26 of them in the fourth quarter, for a 36–20 victory. It was Philadelphia's first playoff win since the 1980 team's NFC Championship Game victory. It was also the Eagles' first road playoff win since the 1949 NFL Championship Game. Cunningham threw two touchdown

REGGIE WHITE

Reggie White became an ordained Baptist minister at the age of 17 while growing up in Tennessee. By the time he left the University of Tennessee on his way to a pro football career, White was known as "The Minister of Defense."

White got a late start on his NFL career because he spent his first two pro seasons with the United States Football League. The league went out of business in 1985. White made his debut with the Eagles in the fourth week of the 1985 season and had an immediate impact. He was named NFL Defensive Rookie of the Year.

White went on to earn Defensive Player of the Year honors for the Eagles in 1987 and for the Green Bay Packers in 1998. He retired as the NFL career sacks leader with 198. Sadly, the Pro Football Hall of Famer died suddenly of a heart attack the day after Christmas in 2004 at the age of 43.

passes to Fred Barnett. The Philadelphia quarterback wowed the entire league with his athleticism. *Sports Illustrated* put Cunningham on the cover of its magazine. The headline read "The Ultimate Weapon."

After two down years, the Eagles were back in the playoffs under Rhodes. That gave Philadelphia six playoff appearances in nine years. The 1995 team opened a 51–7 lead on the Detroit Lions in the third quarter of a 58–37 playoff victory. But the Eagles fell to the Dallas Cowboys a week later.

Randall Cunningham, shown in 1992, played quarterback for the Eagles from 1985 to 1995 and was known for his ability to run as well as pass.

The Eagles again lost their starting quarterback in 1996 when Rodney Peete hurt his knee. Ty Detmer took over and led Philadelphia to four straight wins and a playoff berth with a 10–6 record. However, the 49ers ended the Eagles' season with a 14–0 win in a wild-card playoff game in the rain in San Francisco.

Quarterback Donovan McNabb poses with his family after Philadelphia drafted him in 1999. Many Eagles fans booed the pick.

The Eagles held the second overall pick in the 1999 NFL Draft. Some of the team's fans thought that the pick should be used on Heisman Trophy-winning running back Ricky Williams. When NFL commissioner Paul Tagliabue announced that the Eagles had selected quarterback Donovan McNabb, the team's fans in attendance at New York's Madison Square Garden booed loudly.

But those Eagles fans would be proven wrong. First-year coach Andy Reid believed McNabb had the unique skills needed to run the Eagles' offense. That proved to be the case. Reid would win more games than any other Eagles coach, and McNabb would set most team passing records before he was through.

ANDY REID

Andy Reid took over as Philadelphia's coach after the team went 3–13 in 1998. Reid was twice named NFL Coach of the Year in Philadelphia. He led the Eagles to five NFC Championship Games and one Super Bowl. In 2013 he was named the Kansas City Chiefs head coach. He helped Kansas City to the playoffs in five of his first six seasons there.

The Eagles began the 2000s as one of the best teams in the NFL. However, even though they won 34 regular-season games between 2000 and 2002, they lost in the NFC Championship Game each year. But they finally broke through with a long-awaited run to the Super Bowl after the 2004 season.

CHAPTER 5

THE ROAD TO THE TOP

The Eagles laid the groundwork for their NFC championship before the 2004 season started. They signed defensive end Jevon Kearse and traded for wide receiver Terrell Owens. Donovan McNabb went out and had his best season as a pro. He became the first NFL quarterback to throw more than 30 touchdown passes with fewer than 10 interceptions in the same season as Philadelphia posted a 13–3 record.

The Eagles breezed into the Super Bowl with a pair of easy playoff victories, giving them a shot at the defending champion New England Patriots in Super Bowl XXXIX. However, New England forced four turnovers, and Patriots wide receiver Deion Branch was chosen as the game's MVP after catching 11 passes for 133 yards as the Pats won 24–21.

Andy Reid and Donovan McNabb led the Eagles to many victories but did not win the Super Bowl.

EAGLES
5

DONOVAN MCNABB

Donovan McNabb was a two-sport standout at Syracuse University. He excelled in football at Syracuse and also performed well for the school's powerhouse basketball program.

In the NFL, McNabb ran better than most quarterbacks and quickly became an effective passer on the professional level. Only John Elway, Fran Tarkenton, and Steve Young have matched McNabb's accomplishment of passing for more than 30,000 yards and 200 touchdowns while running for more than 3,000 yards and 20 touchdowns. Through the 2018 season, the six-time Pro Bowl selection held many of the Eagles' all-time passing records.

In April 2010, the Eagles traded McNabb to Washington. He played only one season there before finishing his career with the Minnesota Vikings in 2011. McNabb retired after that season.

But the Eagles had their chances. McNabb hit Greg Lewis for a 30-yard touchdown with 1:48 left. The Eagles got the ball back at their 4-yard line with 46 seconds remaining. However, McNabb was intercepted on the series' third play, ending any hopes of a comeback win.

Philadelphia made the playoffs in eight of 10 seasons during that decade and reached the NFC title game one more time, losing at Arizona in January 2009. But with the new decade on the horizon, the Eagles made a big decision. On April 4, 2010, Philadelphia traded McNabb to Washington.

"While it has been my goal to win a Super Bowl in Philadelphia, we came up short. I enjoyed my 11 years and know we shared a lot more good times than bad," McNabb said in a statement after the trade.

Philadelphia cycled through a handful of quarterbacks attempting to replace McNabb. Untested draft picks Kevin Kolb and Nick Foles, as well as veterans Michael Vick, Mark Sanchez, and Sam Bradford, all got a chance over the next six years. But the Eagles only made the playoffs twice in that span, losing in the wild-card game both times.

Reid was fired after the 2012 season. In 14 years with the Eagles, Reid won more games than any other head coach in team history.

The Eagles found temporary success under new head coach Chip Kelly in 2013. Kelly came from the University of Oregon where his teams used a lot of quick players and scored a lot of points. Kelly tried a similar approach in Philadelphia with Foles, running back LeSean McCoy, and DeSean Jackson. It worked in Kelly's first season. Foles and the Eagles put up the second-most yards per game in the NFL as they went 10–6 and made the playoffs. Once again, however, Philadelphia came up short, losing to the Saints on a last-second field goal in the first round.

Kelly wouldn't last long in Philadelphia. After going 10–6 but missing the playoffs in 2014, the Eagles went 7–9 in 2015 and Kelly was fired with one game left in the disappointing season. He finished with a record of 26–21 in Philadelphia.

After two straight seasons of missing the playoffs, the Eagles brought in offensive guru Doug Pederson in 2016 and selected quarterback Carson Wentz with the second pick in that year's NFL Draft. Wentz started strong, and the Eagles played solid defense. However, it wasn't enough as they went 7–9 and finished last in the NFC East.

Philadelphia went into 2017 with confidence that Wentz and a strong defense could lead the Eagles to a title. And that's exactly what happened. Philadelphia finished an NFC-best 13–3 despite losing Wentz to a season-ending injury in December. Though Foles struggled in relief at first, the defense kept the Eagles competitive, and the quarterback stepped up when it counted. Foles led the Eagles all the way to the Super Bowl LII crown and was named the game's MVP.

With Wentz recovering from his knee injury early in 2018, Foles played two more games before Wentz came back as

LeSean McCoy became the Eagles' all-time leading rusher in 2014.

the starter. In his first five games, Wentz threw 10 touchdown passes and just one interception while averaging 300 passing yards per game.

However, the team wasn't winning. The Eagles went 2–3 in that span, then split their next six games. After an overtime loss in Dallas dropped Philadelphia's record to 6–7, Wentz was diagnosed with a stress fracture in his back. Though Wentz wanted to try to play through the injury, Pederson knew he had a proven veteran as a backup, so he turned to Foles once again.

The next week, the Eagles traveled to Los Angeles to face the Rams on national television. The Rams came into the game 11–2 and were a two-touchdown favorite to beat the Eagles. But Foles wasn't fazed. He threw for 270 yards and the Eagles pulled off a 30–23 upset.

That touched off another string of victories. Facing Houston at home the next week, Foles threw four touchdown passes, but the defense blew a 13-point fourth-quarter lead. No problem. Taking over at his own 11-yard line with two minutes to play, Foles marched the Eagles 72 yards in 10 plays. That set up Jake Elliott's 35-yard field goal as time expired, giving Philadelphia a 32–30 victory. A week later, the defense smothered Washington in a 24–0 win, and when the Minnesota Vikings lost to the Chicago Bears, the Eagles clinched the final playoff spot in the NFC.

Their reward was a trip to Chicago to face the stingy Bears defense. Trailing 15–10 late in the fourth quarter, Foles led another big drive, hitting Golden Tate on a 2-yard touchdown pass to take a 16–15 lead with 56 seconds to play. The Bears fought back, but their potential game-winning field goal hit the left upright and the Eagles held on to win.

Eagles fans hoped young quarterback Carson Wentz had the team heading in the right direction.

Philadelphia's luck finally ran out the following week in New Orleans. The Eagles took a 14–0 lead, but the Saints came back to score the game's final 20 points and pulled out a 20–14 victory. It wasn't another trip to the Super Bowl, but the Eagles certainly gave their fans a lot to cheer about in 2018.

TIMELINE

1933

The Frankford Yellow Jackets move from the Philadelphia suburbs into the city and are renamed the Philadelphia Eagles.

1939

The host Brooklyn Dodgers beat the Eagles 23–14 on October 22 in the first televised NFL game.

1943

Due to a player shortage caused by World War II, the Eagles and Pittsburgh Steelers combine for one season as the Phil-Pitt Steagles.

1947

The Eagles reach the NFL Championship Game but lose to the Chicago Cardinals 28–21 on December 28.

1948

On December 19, Philadelphia wins a NFL Championship Game rematch with the Cardinals 7–0.

1949

The Eagles follow up an 11–1 regular season by blanking the Los Angeles Rams 14–0 in the NFL Championship Game on December 18.

1958

Norm Van Brocklin arrives via a trade with the Rams and takes over as the Eagles' starting quarterback.

1960

Van Brocklin wins the NFL MVP Award and Philadelphia beats the Green Bay Packers 17–13 on December 26.

1961

The Eagles fall short of winning the East Division and getting a shot to defend their title.

1978

On November 19, "the Miracle at the Meadowlands" helps the Eagles end a 17-year playoff drought.

1981
Philadelphia loses 27–10 to the Oakland Raiders on January 25 in its first Super Bowl appearance.

1988
The Eagles lose the "Fog Bowl" to the Bears on December 31 in Chicago.

1992
On June 25, Philadelphia standout defensive tackle Jerome Brown dies in an automobile accident in Florida.

1999
Eagles fans at Madison Square Garden boo when the team selects quarterback Donovan McNabb second overall in the NFL Draft on April 17.

2005
On February 6, the Eagles fall 24–21 to the New England Patriots in Super Bowl XXXIX.

2009
On January 18, the Arizona Cardinals defeat the Eagles 32–25, Philadelphia's fourth loss in five tries in the NFC Championship Game this decade.

2010
On April 4, the Eagles trade McNabb to Washington for two draft picks.

2016
Philadelphia trades up to select quarterback Carson Wentz with the second pick of the NFL Draft.

2018
Backup quarterback Nick Foles leads the Eagles to their first Super Bowl victory, defeating the Patriots 41–33 on February 4.

2018
The Eagles sneak into the playoffs on the last day of the season but can't repeat their Super Bowl success.

QUICK STATS

FRANCHISE HISTORY

Philadelphia Eagles (1933–42, 1944–)
Phil-Pitt Steagles (1943)

SUPER BOWLS *(wins in bold)*

1980 (XV), 2004 (XXXIX), **2017 (LII)**

NFL CHAMPIONSHIP GAMES (1933–69, *wins in bold*)

1947, **1948**, **1949**, **1960**

NFC CHAMPIONSHIP GAMES *(since 1970 AFL-NFL merger)*

1980, 2001, 2002, 2003, 2004, 2008, 2017

DIVISIONCHAMPIONSHIPS *(since 1970 AFL-NFL merger)*

1980, 1988, 2001, 2002, 2003, 2004, 2006, 2010, 2013, 2017

KEY COACHES

Earle "Greasy" Neale (1941–50): 63–43–5, 3–1 (playoffs)
Andy Reid (1999–2012): 130–93–1, 10–9 (playoffs)

KEY PLAYERS *(position, seasons with team)*

Chuck Bednarik (C/LB, 1949–62)
Harold Carmichael (WR, 1971–83)
Fletcher Cox (DL, 2012–)
Randall Cunningham (QB, 1985–95)
Brian Dawkins (DB, 1996–2008)
Nick Foles (QB, 2012–14, 2017–)
Ron Jaworski (QB, 1977–86)
Sonny Jurgensen (QB, 1957–63)
Tommy McDonald (WR, 1957–63)
Donovan McNabb (QB, 1999–2009)
Pete Pihos (TE/DE, 1947–55)
Tra Thomas (OT, 1998–2008)
Steve Van Buren (RB, 1944–51)
Carson Wentz (QB, 2016–)
Brian Westbrook (RB, 2002–09)
Reggie White (DE, 1985–92)

HOME FIELDS

Lincoln Financial Field (2003–)
Veterans Stadium (1971–2002)
Franklin Field (1958–70)
Shibe Park (1940–57)
Municipal Stadium (1936–39)
Baker Bowl (1933–35)

*All statistics through 2018 season

QUOTES AND ANECDOTES

To be a quarterback in this league you've got to be stuck in the middle in that locker room, looking at those guys, and at the same time be able to handle the head coach and management and so on. You're juggling a lot of balls there, and so that's a tough thing—a tremendously tough thing to do and do it well. I thought Donovan did that as well as anybody.

—Andy Reid on Donovan McNabb

The Eagles and the host Brooklyn Dodgers played in the first televised NFL game on October 22, 1939. NBC made the game available to the approximately 1,000 television sets in existence in New York City.

Eagles all-time leading receiver Harold Carmichael set an NFL record when he caught a pass in his 106th consecutive game in 1979. The 6-foot-8 wide receiver increased the record, which has since been broken, to 127 games. It was stopped when he suffered a back injury in the final game of the 1980 season against the Dallas Cowboys.

Even though Philadelphia was the top seed in the NFC in the playoffs in January 2018, the Eagles were considered underdogs without injured starting quarterback Carson Wentz. Philadelphia tried to use its underdog status as a way to get motivated to win. Defensive lineman Chris Long and other players wore dog masks during the playoffs to signify that they enjoyed being the underdogs. Fans started wearing masks too, and the Eagles ended up winning the Super Bowl.

GLOSSARY

All-Pro
An award given to the top players at their position regardless of their conference. It is a high honor, as there are fewer spots on the All-Pro team than on the Pro Bowl teams.

berth
A place, spot, or position, such as in the NFL playoffs.

comeback
When a team losing a game rallies to tie the score or take the lead.

commissioner
The chief executive of a sports league.

coordinator
An assistant coach who is in charge of the offense or defense.

dominant
The player or team that proves to be consistently better than the opponent.

draft
A system that allows teams to acquire new players coming into a league.

enshrine
To put in an honored place, such as the Pro Football Hall of Fame.

franchise
A sports organization, including the top-level team and all minor league affiliates.

linebacker
A player who usually lines up behind the defensive linemen and in front of the defensive backs.

postseason
Games played in the playoffs by the top teams after the regular season schedule has been completed.

rookie
A professional athlete in his or her first year of competition.

MORE INFORMATION

BOOKS

DiPrimio, Pete. *Carson Wentz*. Kennett Square, PA: Purple Toad Publishing, Inc., 2019.

Graves, Will. *Philadelphia Eagles*. Minneapolis, MN: Abdo Publishing, 2017.

Lajiness, Katie. *Philadelphia Eagles*. Minneapolis, MN: Abdo Publishing, 2017.

ONLINE RESOURCES

Booklinks
NONFICTION NETWORK
FREE! ONLINE NONFICTION RESOURCES

To learn more about the Philadelphia Eagles, visit **abdobooklinks.com** or scan this QR code. These links are routinely monitored and updated to provide the most current information available.

PLACES TO VISIT

Lincoln Financial Field
1 Lincoln Financial Field Way
Philadelphia, PA 19148
215-463-5500
lincolnfinancialfield.com

The stadium has been the venue for Eagles home games since 2003. It also hosts Temple University football games.

NovaCare Complex
1 Novacare Way
Philadelphia, PA 19145
215-463-2500
philadelphiaeagles.com/new/training-camp

This is the home of the Eagles' team offices and training camp

INDEX

ABOUT THE AUTHOR

Robert Cooper is a retired law enforcement officer and lifelong NFL fan. He and his wife live in Seattle near their only son and two grandchildren.